POSITION
OF THE DAY

POSITION
OF THE DAY

SEX EVERY DAY
IN EVERY WAY

FROM NERVE.COM

CHRONICLE BOOKS

SAN FRANCISCO

Library of Congress Cataloging-in-Publication Data available.
ISBN: 0-8118-3957-5

Manufactured in Canada

Designed by Venus D'Amore

Distributed in Canada by Raincoast Books
9050 Shaughnessy Street
Vancouver, British Columbia V6P 6E5

20 19 18 17

Chronicle Books LLC
85 Second Street
San Francisco, California 94105
www.chroniclebooks.com

INTRODUCTION

>

When we started publishing the Position of the Day on Nerve.com, it never occurred to us that couples would actually try these positions. We were more interested in coming up with clever names than dishing practical sex advice. Take "Keeping Up with the Joneses," for example (June 4) — even if you did happen to own a rocking chair, you'd have to be an idiot (or a member of Cirque du Soleil) to attempt intercourse in this position. It's all about name-dropping. Or so we thought.

But our resourceful readers had other ideas, and they started regaling us with tales of their attempts of "climbing Mount Pleasant" (June 16; fortunately, none of them sent pictures). Some wanted us to rate positions for difficulty (perhaps so they could brag to the Joneses?), others got offended when we included positions that were obviously impossible (like "The Quasimodo," April 23), and still others wondered how they were expected to get by on only one new position a day.

Perhaps it was the silly nicknames that made the positions — and actually bringing them into play — seem more like a game than work. Couples are often loath to consult hippie sex manuals for "inspiration" because it's like admitting that there's something wrong, that something needs to be fixed, that the so-called "spark" is gone. But it's nothing to be ashamed of — we all become creatures of habit at some point. Hey, orgasms are good things, and sometimes you just want to take the shortest route to your happy place. But even "The Happy Landing" (June 25) can get boring if that's all you do. And half the fun of an orgasm is the journey there. How's that for "inspiration"?

But this isn't a hippie sex manual, damn it, and we don't have any interest in fixing sex — which perhaps makes Nerve a better source for higher learning. We're not telling you the way sex should be, we're just providing the raw material for your own interpretation. Plus, you don't have to beat yourself up if you can't master all these positions because a third of them are impossible anyway. (Or a quarter if you stretch first.)

Think of this book as a preemptive strike — why wait 'til you're in the dreaded rut and actually need one of those hippie manuals to swing from the rafters and yell, "I can see my house from here!" (August 20). The moment you think you know all there is to know about sex is the moment your sex life is over. The first step is admitting you need help. The second step is admitting you need this book. The third step is buying it.

— Em and Lo, Near-Experts, Nerve.com

THE POSITIONS

>

HAPPY NEW YEAR

THE MUD FLAP

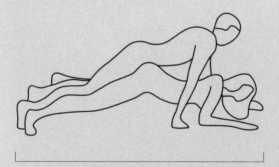

THE DROP AND GIVE ME 20

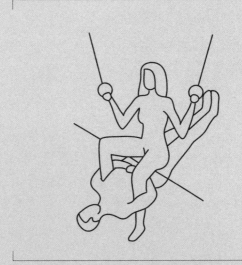

THE GYM MEMBERSHIP

THE REAR ADMIRAL

EXCUSE ME, DO I KNOW YOU?

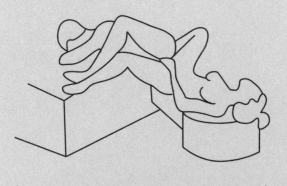

WHOSE LEG IS IT ANYWAY?

WALK LIKE AN EGYPTIAN

THE CHRYSALIS

THE GETTING TO KNOW YOU

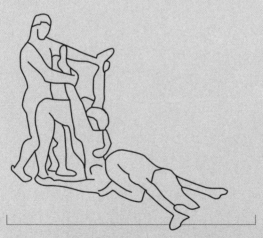

THE WELL-OILED MACHINE

THE BETTY ROCKER

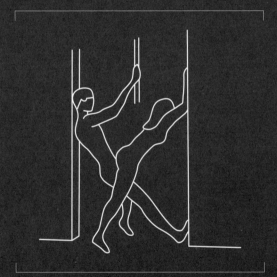

YOU RANG?

THE BI-POLE-HER

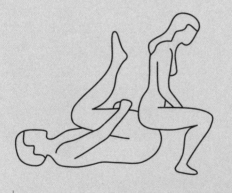

GOING CAMPING

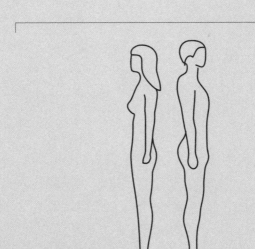

THE HEADACHE

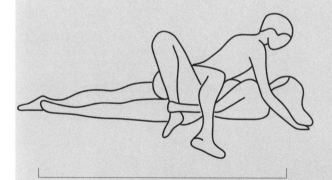

THE HAMSTRING SANDWICH

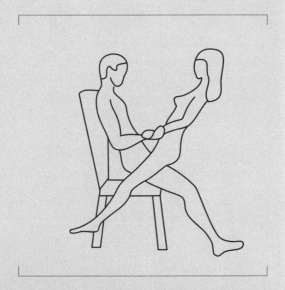

THE TEETER-TOTTER

THE JUNGLE JIM

THE HAPPY FIREMAN

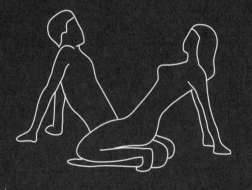

THE MICKEY D'S

THE HOME STRETCH

HARVEY, THE WALLBANGER

ONE SAUSAGE WRAP, TO GO

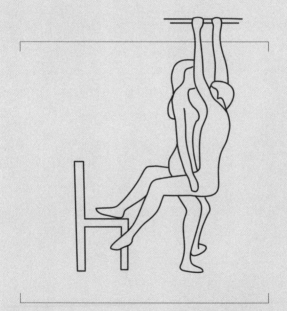

THE MEAT HOOK

TORVILLE AND DEAN

THE AMBUSH

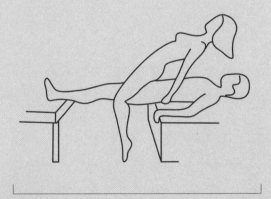

THE MOTION SIMULATION RIDE

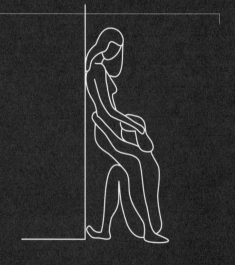

THE DOWN COMFORTER

THE CORPORATE MERGER

THE TUNNEL OF LOVE

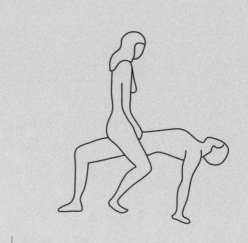

THE LADY GODIVA

WHAT ARE YOU, MY SHADOW?

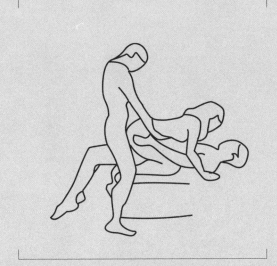

THE POSTMAN ALWAYS RINGS TWICE

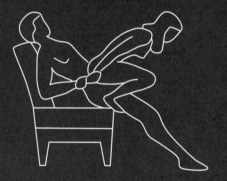

THE STARTING BLOCK

HELPING YOUR FRIEND MOVE

UNDER THE HOOD

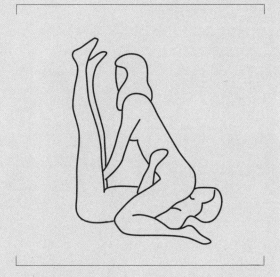

THE BOTTOM FEEDER

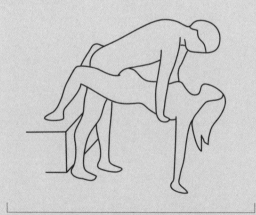

THE SCARLETT AND RHETT

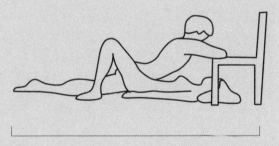

THE REUPHOLST-HER

THE HALF HITCH

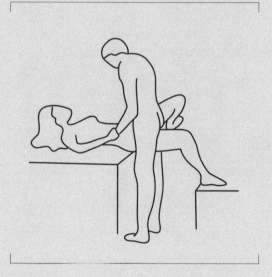

SEXUAL HEELING

THE LINCOLN DOUGLAS

AUSTRALIAN FOR SEX

THE HALLMARK MOMENT

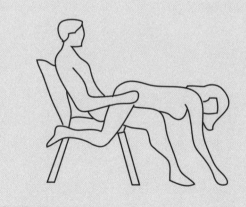

THE BACK SEAT DRIVER

THE FLYING BUTT PLIERS

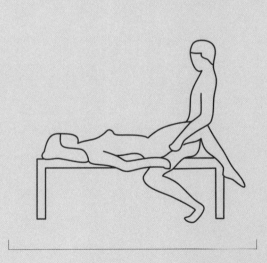

THE PLEDGE

THE SOCKET TO HER

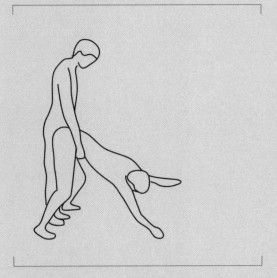

THE EMPIRE STRIKES FROM THE BACK

THE HEISMAN

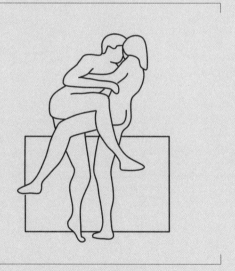

THE SUMO

THE KNEE HIGH

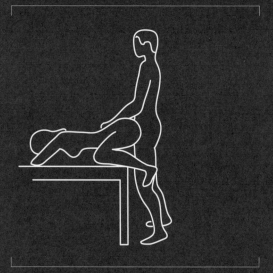

THE CUSTOMS OFFICER

MY, WHAT A BIG SWING YOU HAVE

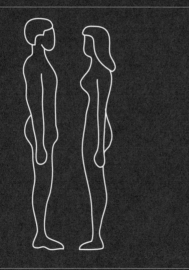

THE MORRISSEY

CAN'T YOU SEE I'M TRYING TO WATCH THE GAME?

THE PRINCESS AND THE P. . .

THE DOOR JAM

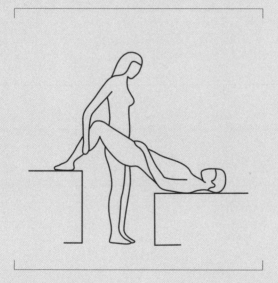

HELLO, NURSE!

THE ABDOMINIZER

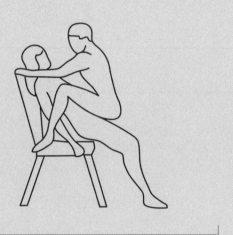

IT'S TIME FOR MY WALK

THE TWINKIE

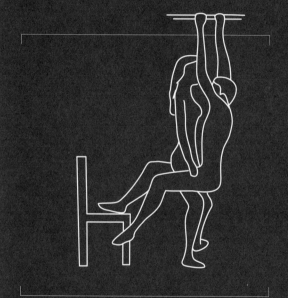

THE HUNGMAN

THE CHAIN OF FOOLS

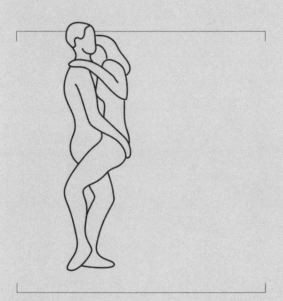

LAVATORY OCCUPIED

SITTING ON TOP OF THE WORLD

GLADIATOR

THE CONSOLATION

THE PROBLEM WITH YOGA

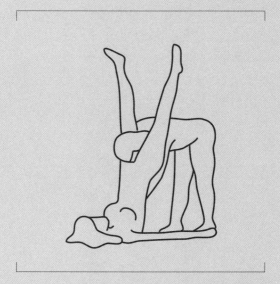

THE BIRDFEEDER

OLD RELIABLE

THE HOVERCRAFT

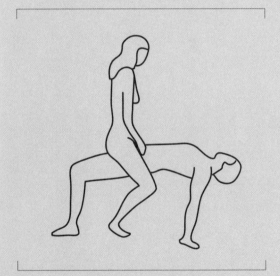

THE TABLE DANCE

THE FOSSE

FINDING HER FOUR-LEAF CLOVER

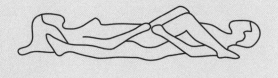

THE BADLANDS

THE LEG WARMER

THE TAILFEATHER

BENCH WARMERS

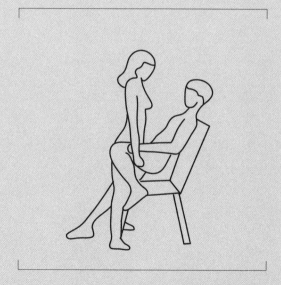

THE STANDING O

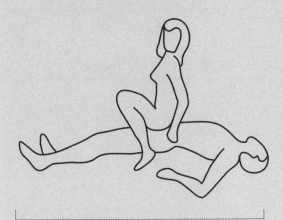

SIT & SPIN

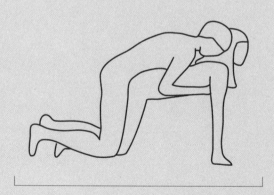

THE HUMPBACK WAIL

THE PRUDE AWAKENING

THE MOTION OF THE OCEAN

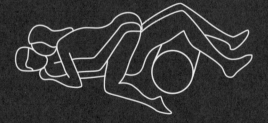

THE CRAFTMATIC

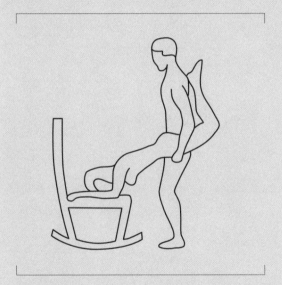

THE NOSE DIVE

BASIC INSTINCT

THE PILE DRIVER

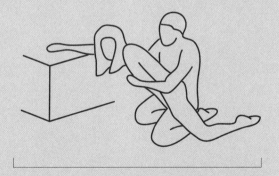

HUGGER MUGGER

THE LINDA HAMILTON

THE TADPOLE

THE PORT-O-HOTTIE

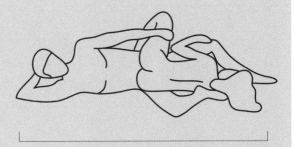

THE DOUBLE HELIX

STRICTLY BEDROOM

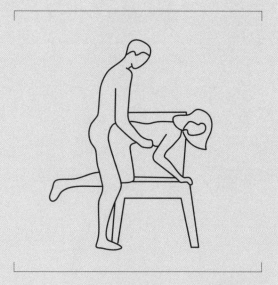

THE HOT SEAT

THE DISMOUNT

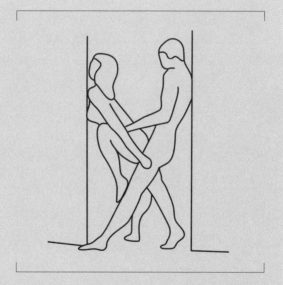

THE NOSE JOB

LOOKING FOR LOOSE CHANGE

PULL OUTS

THE BACKSTAB

THE RICKSHAW

THE BEGINNER'S SWIMMING LESSON

THE JAWS OF LIFE

THE BRICKLAYER

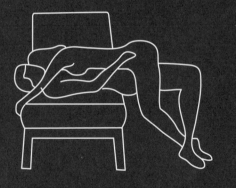

LOOK MA, NO WET SPOT

THE MORK HANDSHAKE

THE DRILL BIT

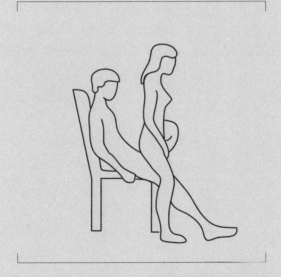

IS THIS SEAT TAKEN?

THE MUZZLE

THE QUASIMODO

THIS IS THE WAY THE LADIES RIDE

90 AND RISING

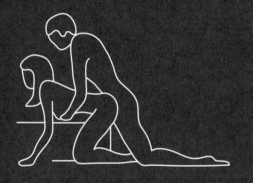

THE HEIMLICH

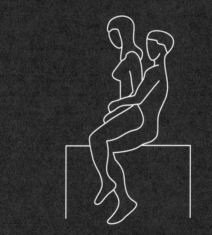

A BIRD IN THE HAND. . .

THE DURGA

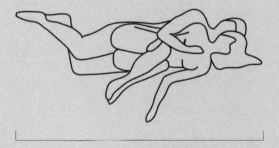

THE STOP, DROP & ROLL

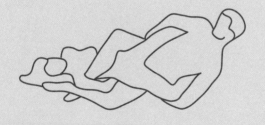

THE ESCHER

THE MAY POLE

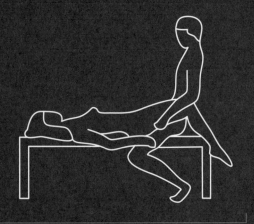

THE COFFEE TABLE HOOK

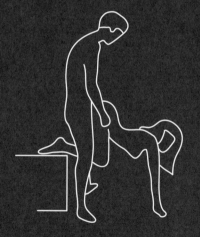

POKING THE INCHWORM WITH A STICK

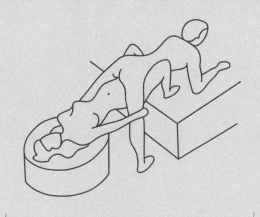

MISSIONARY IMPOSSIBLE

GUM INSPECTION

THE FUN HOUSE MIRROR

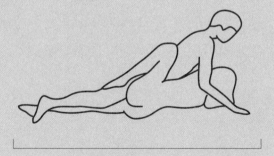

THE SIDE BEEF

THE INTERMEDIATE SWIMMING LESSON

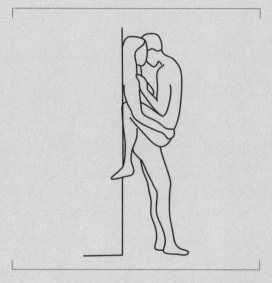

I WANT MY MOMMY

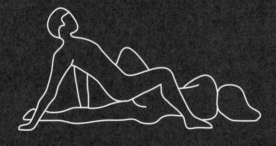

THE MALE MUD FLAP.

THE DOUBLEMINT

ROCK A THIGH BABY

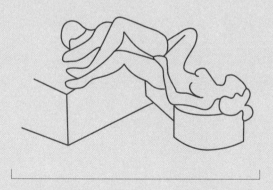

HOMEBIRTHING

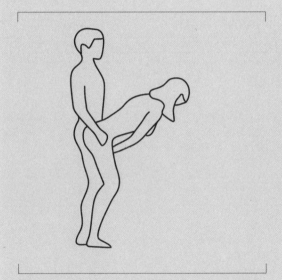

HIDING THE SALAMI

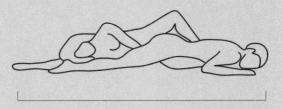

THE NARCOLEPTICS

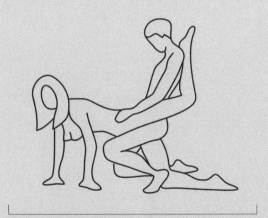

THE HIGH HEEL

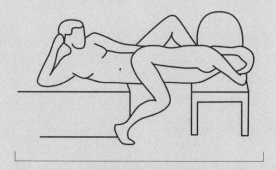

THE MICHELANGELO

THE TWO-HUMPED DROMEDARY

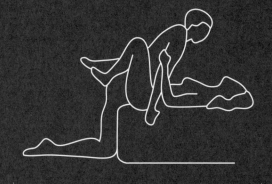

THE SMOOTH TALKER

THE SIXTY EIGHT

DOUBLECLICKING

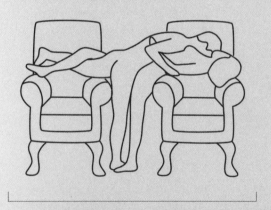

THE TWO-CHAIR SNARE

THE EARTHQUAKE

THE CIRQUE DU SOLEIL

WHAT'S GOOD FOR THE GOOSE...

THE NOT SO FAST, MISTER

THE ASSASSIN

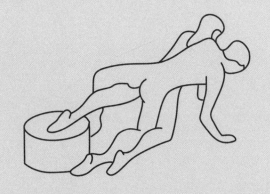

MR. & MRS. CLEAN

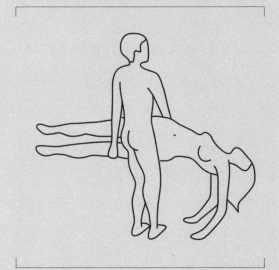

THE MARTHA GRAHAM TRYOUT

THE STARING CONTEST

THE OLD TACK ON THE SEAT TRICK

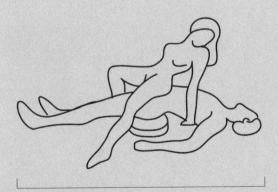

THE STEALTH BOMBSHELL

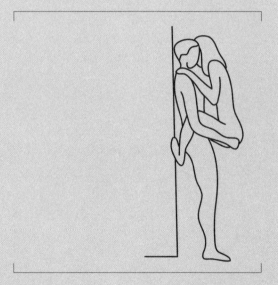

THE ELECTRA COMPLEX

THE CRAFTY CHIROPRACTOR

KEEPING UP WITH THE JONESES

THE ROLLING PIN

THE SLINGSHOT

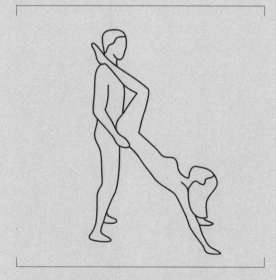

THE BEST OF TIMES, THE WORST OF TIMES

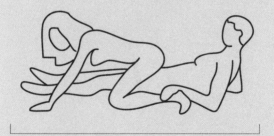

YOU GIVE ME FEMUR

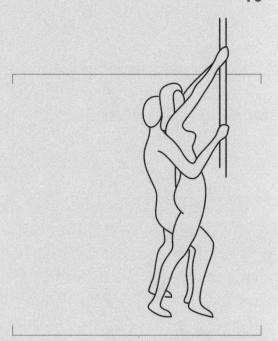

TARZAN, MEET JANE

SO YOU LIKED THE LASAGNA...

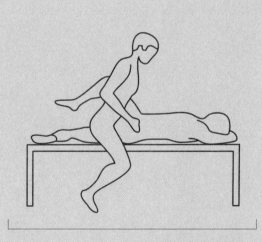

THE PHYSICAL THERAPIST

THE GLAZED TWIST

RAISING HER FLAG

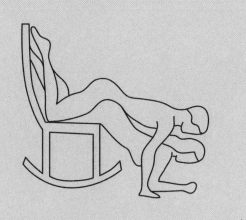

THE SLINKY

CLIMBING MOUNT PLEASANT

THE COOL HAND LUKE

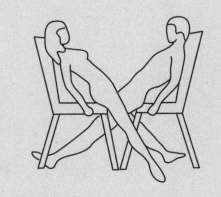

REGENERATION X

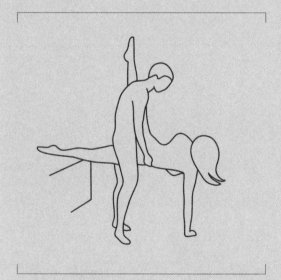

THE ESTHER WILLIAMS

DADDY'S HOME

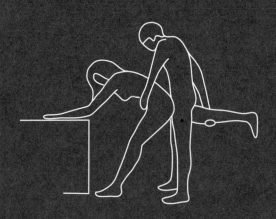

THE HURDLE

THE SUPER GLUE

THE CRULLER

THE SPRINGBOARD

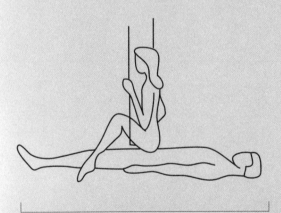

THE HAPPY LANDING

ROCK, DON'T CRY, BABY

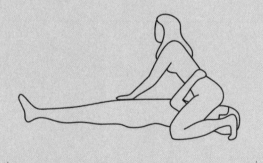

ON YOUR MARK!

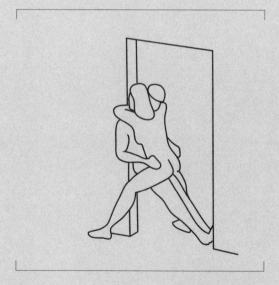

IMMORAL SUPPORT

THE FIRE HYDRANT

THE REUNION

OHHHHH, CANADA!

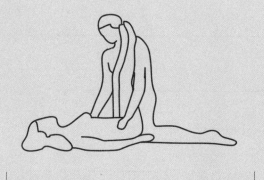

THE FOLDING MABLE

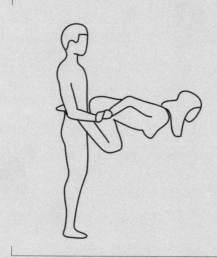

BOMBS BURSTING IN AIR

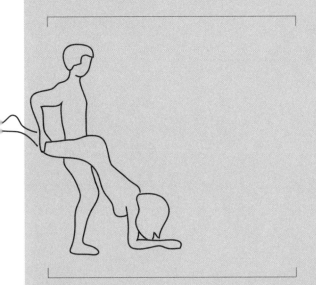

THE HOOVHER

THE VIEW

THE CAT'S CRADLE

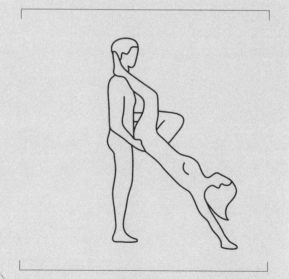

THE SUNDIAL

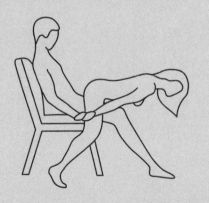

THE CRASH POSITION

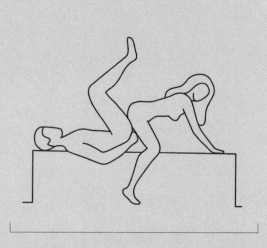

THE SHURIKEN

ADDITION

THE HOKEY POKEY

THE MANWICH

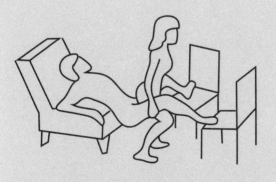

THE IKEA SALE

THE YOGA INSTRUCTOR

GIVE ME A "U"

THE GRAVITRON

THEPRESSEDSANDWICH

DEEP HEELING

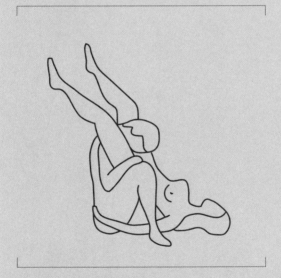

THE MADAME CURIE

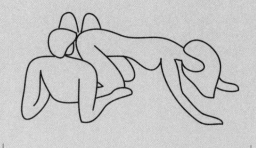

PIN THE TAIL ON THE GIRLFRIEND

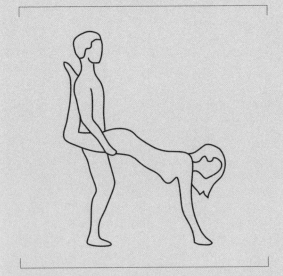

PUSH INS

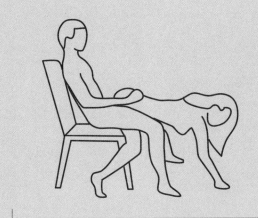

TV DINNER

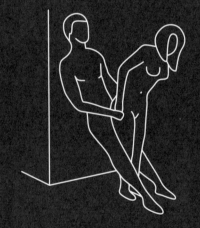

THE WEDGIE

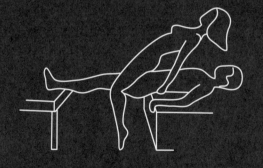

THE MACH 3

CHAIRWAY TO HEAVEN

THE FALSE START

THE PRAYING MANTIS

THE STICK SHIFT

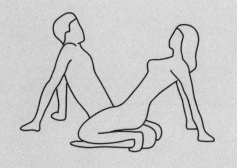

THE GRAND TETON

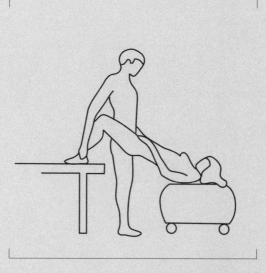

THE 4:30

THE BUTTERFLY CHAIR

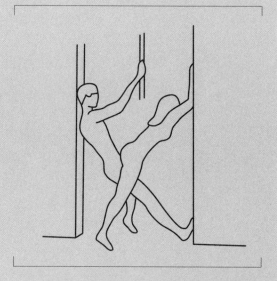

THE LURCH

THE BUTTER CUP

SIT ON IT, MRS. C

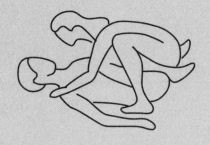

LEAPFROG

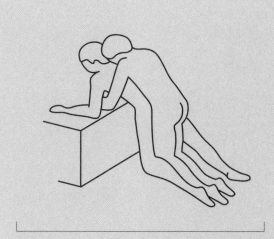

THE WET BLANKET

OOPS!...I DID IT AGAIN

SLIDING DOWN THE BANISTER

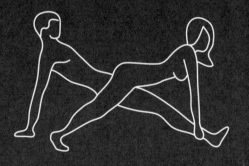

X MARKS THE G-SPOT

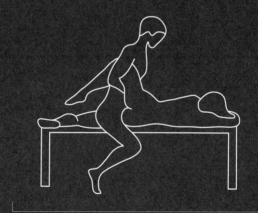

THE LAZY SUSAN

BANGING IN THE BALANCE

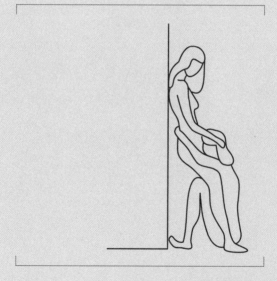

SNORKELING

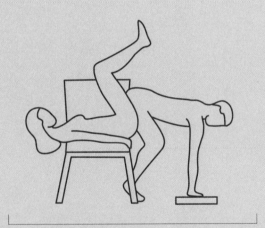

THE SILENT TREATMENT

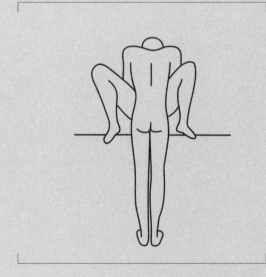

THE PAP TALK

YIN YANG

THE GREASY SPOON

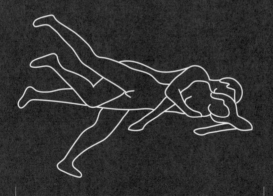

THE SQUID

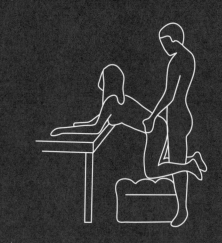

THE OTTOMAN BOTTOMMAN

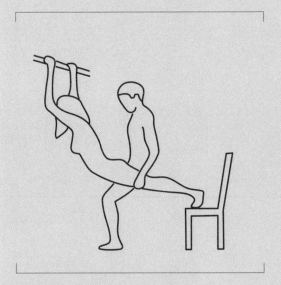

I CAN SEE MY HOUSE FROM HERE

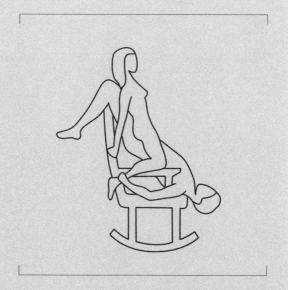

SO WRONG IT'S RIGHT

THE NYPD

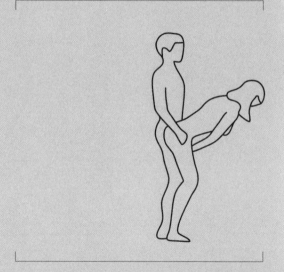

THE LOST KEY

THE THINKER

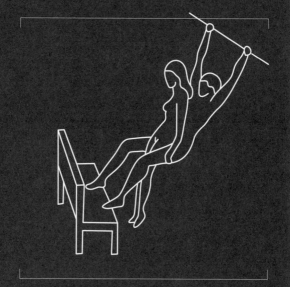

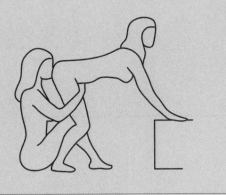

THE THERMOMETER

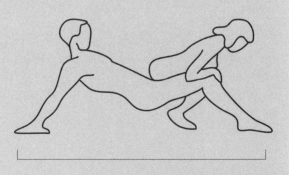

DOWN IN FRONT!

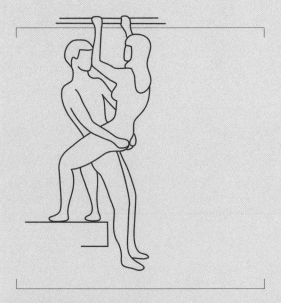

SWING LOW, SWEET CHARIOT

THE GARGOYLE

THE OYSTER, MY WORLD

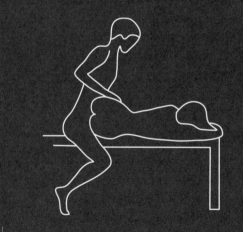

THE DOCTOR PROCTO

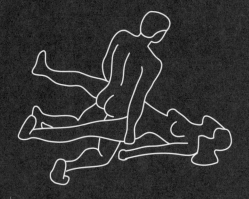

THE DOWSING ROD

THE LEG UP

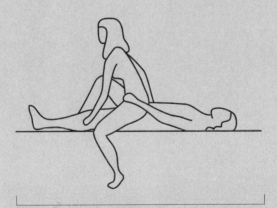

HOPPING THE FENCE

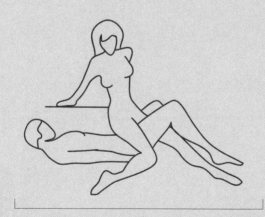

SLIDING INTO HOME

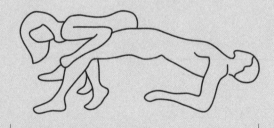

THE PORTAPOTTY

BACK IN THE SADDLE

THE TUG BOAT

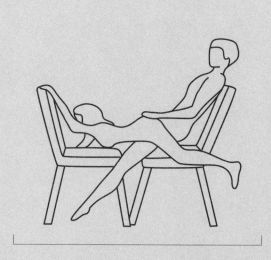

THE LAPTOP

THE KNEE DEEP

THE ONSCREEN KISS

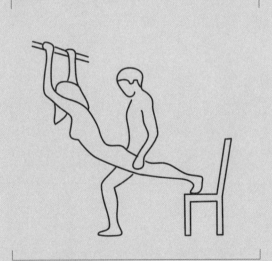

BANG-GLIDING

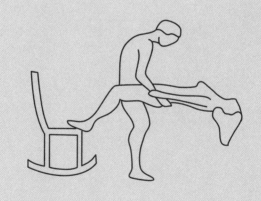

GET OFF YOUR ROCKER

THE LEGGO MY EGGO

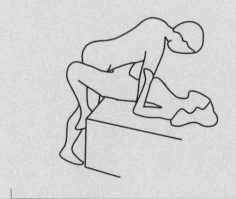

GETTING OFF HER SOAPBOX

THE PEDICURE

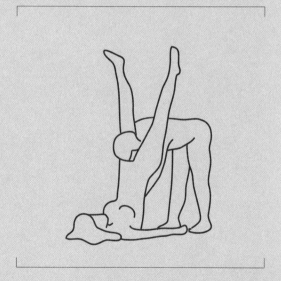

THE VALLEY OF THE DOLL

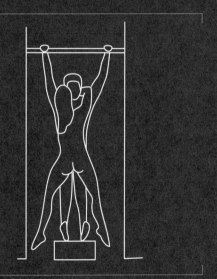

FEELING THE BURN

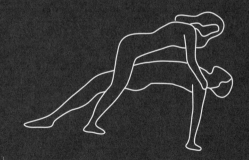

FASTER PUSSYCAT, KILL, KILL

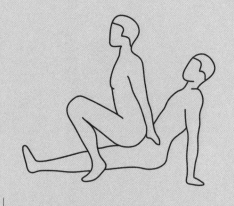

THE LAY-Z-BOYS

THE PRIVATE DANCER

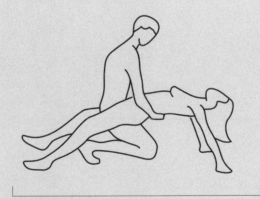

THE DRAMA QUEEN

STUBBORNNESS

THE BIKE PUMP

TAKING THE A TRAIN

THE CARTESIAN CIRCLE

HOME DELIVERY

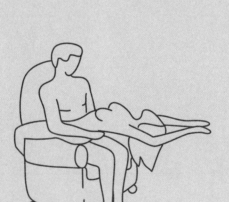

THE REMOTE CONTROL

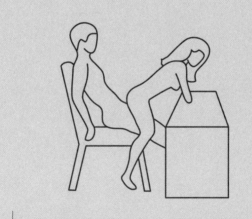

THE HARD BARGAIN

JEDI TRAINING

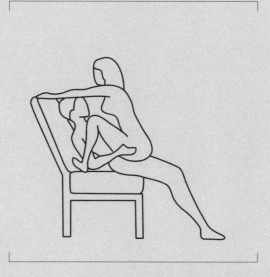

THE COXSWAIN

THE AWKWARD MOMENT

THE GERONIMO

BETWEEN A ROCKER AND A HARD PLACE

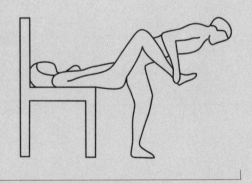

THE NO WAY IN HELL

EROTIC ASPHYXIATION FOR DUMMIES

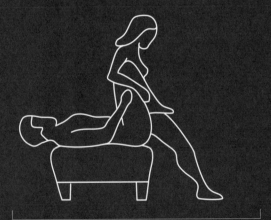

THE T-BAR

THE LONDON BRIDGE

THE SUCCUBUS

GROUP HUG

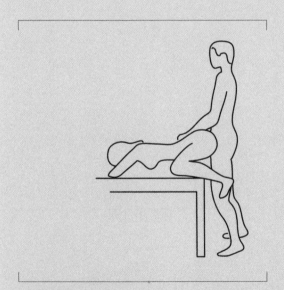

STUFFING HER GOOSE

LAND HO!

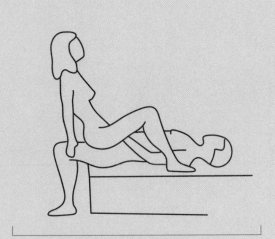

THE HOUSE CALL

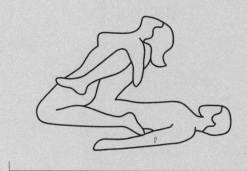

THE REALIGNMENT

THE COASTER

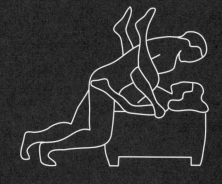

REARRANGING THE FURNITURE

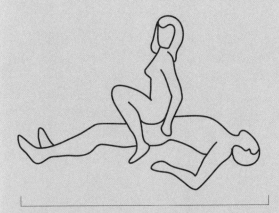

SELF-SERVICE

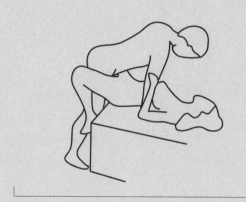

COUNTER SERVICE

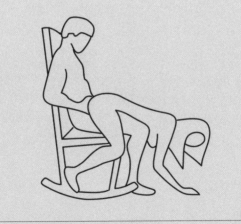

THE LOST CONTACT

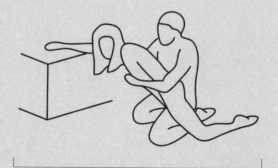

THE BUM WRAP

PETER: I'M FLYING!

THE VITRUVIAN

THE LUMBERJACKS

WORKING HARD

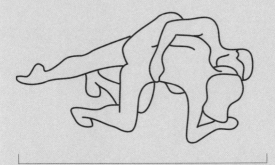

RIGHT FOOT RED

THE BODY SURF

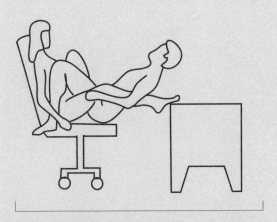

THE SECOND INTERVIEW

GETTIN' IT ON BENDED KNEE

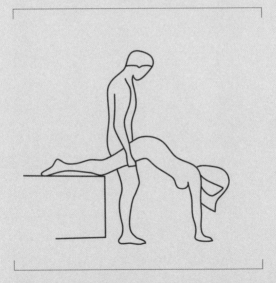

THE PERSONAL TRAINER

THE CLING WRAP

TRICK OR TREAT

THE CUSHION PIN

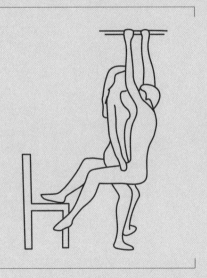

THE HANGING CHAD

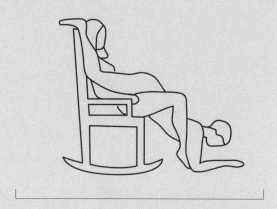

THE CHALLAH

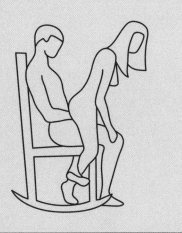

THE MASTER PUPPETEER

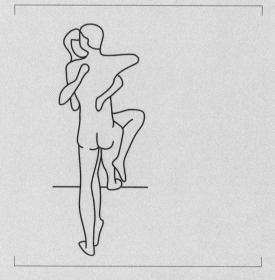

STAIRWAY TO HEAVEN

LIGHT AS A FEATHER...

THE LEANING TOWER OF LISA

THE SWEDISH PUMP

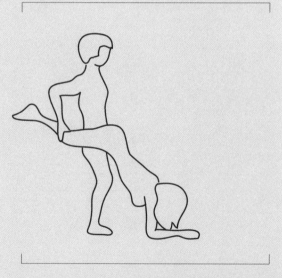

THE SNOW BLOWER

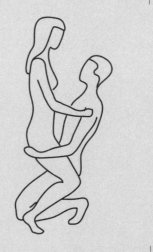

THE ELEVATE-HER

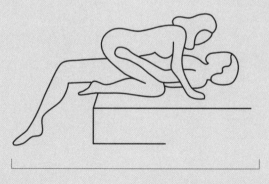

THE CROTCH ROCKET

ROCKING THE CRADLE OF LOVE

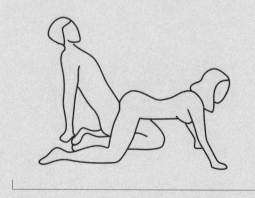

THE BOBSLED

november.) **14**

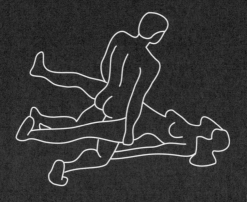

THE SHALLOW GRAVE

MIR TO SPACE SHUTTLE: WE ARE NOT CONNECTING . . .

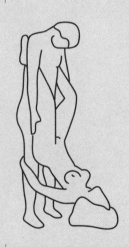

THE SHAKEDOWN

THE SLOW GETAWAY

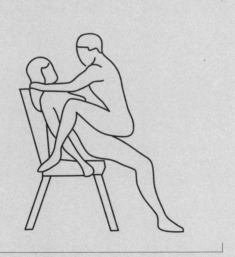

JOCKEYING FOR ATTENTION

IT'S GOOD TO BE KING

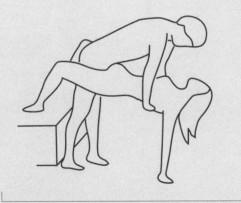

THE DIP STICK

THE MASHED POTATO

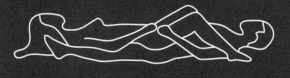

LOW-IMPACT AEROBICS

CHECK PLEASE!

LEVITATING THE LOVELY ASSISTANT

THE MAYFLOWER MASTHEAD

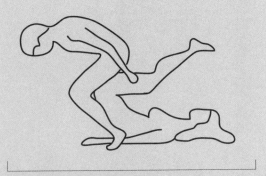

THE ALPINE DOWNHILL

STARGAZING

THE OLD BALLS AND CHAIN

THE STIFF NECKER

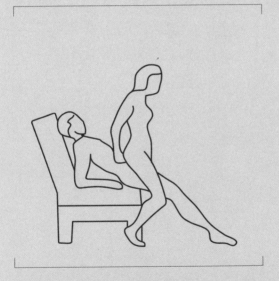

THE WATER SLIDE

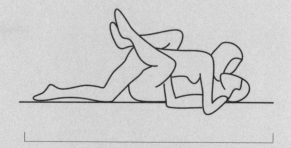

THE AGGRESSIVE FIRST MOVE

THE PROPOSAL

EYE TO EYE

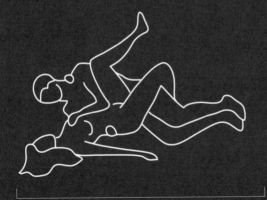

TAKING THE FALL

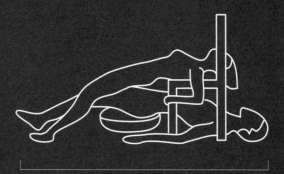

THE CHAIR LIFT

THE ART O' CHOKE

RIDING SIDESADDLE

BETTER THAN EIGHT PRESENTS

THE HOMECOMING

THE SKI LIFT

THE ROCKET LAUNCHER

OCTOPUSSY

THE SERENDIPITOUS TRIP

THE THREE O'CLOCK APPOINTMENT

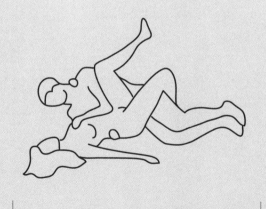

THE DIRTY DIP

THE PUBE CRAWL

THE RAINY DAY

THE PRODIGAL SON

THE GLASS CEILING

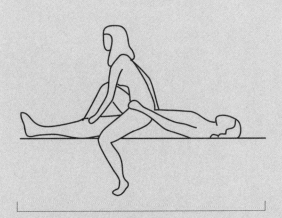

THE FENCE SITTER

THE FOLDING CHAIR

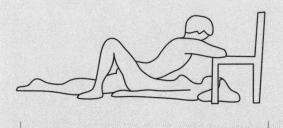

THE CHEAT SEAT

YOU'RE HIRED

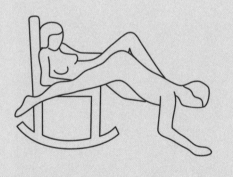

THE NUTCRACKER

SANTA'S HELPER

STACKING THE BOXES

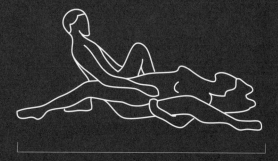

THE ACHILLES

THE PINWHEEL STICK

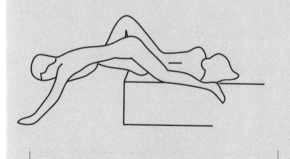

LINKIN' LOGS

THE END IS NEAR

BIO

>

EM & LO (EMMA TAYLOR AND LORELEI SHARKEY)
pen Nerve.com's sex and relationship's advice column,
"The Em & Lo Down (Advice from Near-Experts)."
They are also the authors of *The Big Bang: Nerve's
Guide to the New Sexual Universe.*